T<small>HE</small> L<small>ANGUAGE OF</small> F<small>LOWERS</small>

Marthe Seguin-Fontes

T H E L A N G U A G E
OF F L O W E R S

Sterling Publishing Co., Inc.
New York

Library of Congress Cataloging-in-Publication Data Available

10   9   8   7   6   5   4   3   2   1

Published in 2001 by Sterling Publishing Co., Inc.
387 Park Avenue South, New York, NY 10016

Originally published in France under the title *Le langage des fleurs* by
Éditions du Chêne—Hachette Livre
43 quai de Grenelle, 75905 Paris Cedex 15
© 1995 by Éditions du Chêne—Hachette Livre
English Translation © 2001 by Sterling Publishing
Distributed in Canada by Sterling Publishing
c/o Canadian Manda Group, One Atlantic Avenue, Suite 105
Toronto, Ontario, M6K 3E7, Canada
Distributed in Great Britain and Europe by Cassell PLC
Wellington House, 125 Strand, London WC2R 0BB, England
Distributed in Australia by Capricorn Link (Australia) Pty Ltd.
P.O. Box 704, Windsor, NSW 2756, Australia

Printed in China

Sterling ISBN 0-8069-9073-2

Introduction

Years ago, flowers spoke louder than words, and the most subtle way of expressing an intimate thought was by offering a token blossom or a bouquet of flowers.

The language of flowers, which was actively cultivated like a garden or an art, relied on petals and foliage to convey feeling and emotions instead of words.

The language of flowers is believed to have originated in oriental harems; like precious possessions, women were jealously guarded and had no other means of conveying amorous messages, then taboo, without the sultan or vizier taking note.

In ancient Greece and Rome, flowers were cast in a different light: instead of feelings and emotions, mythology associated them with people—gods, goddesses and others granted access to Mount Olympus. Recurrent patterns and themes included nymphs who turned themselves into flowers to flee lustful gods, or were turned into flowers by the jealous wives of these gods, and thus no longer presented a threat.

In the Middle Ages, flowers were associated with Christianity and Christian symbols. They were used to illustrate legends of saints and monks beset by the devil, who usually appeared as either a monster or dragon that had to be slain. Undaunted by his wounds, God's chosen one succeeded

in slaying the beast, and a flower sprang up from each drop of blood that fell to the earth. The blossom was generally white, a symbol of purity. The Crusaders brought back sagas and tales from the Holy Land about battles fought and blood spilled in the name of the Cross. The cult that flourished around the Blessed Virgin Mary christened her "mystical Rose," while wildflowers were rebaptized with names derived from Our Lady's garments. The latter included the bindweed (Our Lady's nightcap) and digitalis (Our Lady's gloves), as well as an entire collection of naive and religious references.

Minstrels and troubadours reinforced the secular nature of floral connotations. The Floral Games, a kind of poetic joust, was held in Toulouse, with competitors vying for the Golden Violet and the Golden Dogrose.

Popular tradition passed down by oral narratives and songs reveal the many plant-related miracles that took place following the burial of lovers in a single tomb. Honeysuckle flourished on Heloise and Abelard's tomb; elsewhere roses sprang up and vines grew, like in the song "To Lorient the Lovely One" (the vine was so abundant that "three ships were built" from its wood). Thus flourished the tradition of miraculous flowers and plants.

During the Renaissance, ancient mythology made a comeback. The great poets found endless inspiration in floral subjects and write elegies to flowers, particularly wildflowers; English daisies; narcissus; wallflowers; and, of course, the queen of all flowers, the rose.

The language of flowers, however, flourished most abundantly in England after Chaucer translated a portion of *Le Roman de la Rose*. A century later, Shakespeare alluded to floral vocabulary in many plays and sonnets, the best known example being Ophelia's bouquet in *Hamlet*, composed of rosemary, pansies, fennel, columbine, rue, and English daisies. This floral code is less common today, yet England still has a variety of flowers with poetic names, including the hollyhock ("holy hook"), Lady's slipper, and orchids.

Botanical imagery once again grew popular during the nineteenth century. The symbols were recorded in books and anthologies and are still in use today. These include pine trees, holly, and mistletoe heralding the joyous Christmas holidays; clover, on condition that it be four-leafed, for good luck; lily of the valley, a sign of happiness, offered on Mayday; and the gold-embroidered oak-leaf trim on the caps of French generals. So, although more and more people are offering flowers or having them delivered— "Say it with flowers" being one of the more popular advertising slogans—the actual meaning and symbolism of each flower has grown less distinct. They are taken to be tokens of love, friendship, and gratitude, with the individual significance of each flower being blurred. The ecology movement as a backlash against our high-tech industrialized world may revive the language of flowers. Regardless, this botanical stroll through the petals and green, accompanied by poets who have always been ardent lovers of nature, will prove captivating to any reader.

Each stem
Of every flower
Conceals
A thousand words
Be gentle with them.

FUJIWARA NO HIROTSUGU

COLUMBINE

∎

Folly

Caprice

∎

Two blue flowers were blowing in a breeze on a hill
And one said to the other, "I cannot hold still.
I tremble beside you and I feel so confused."
And the other replied, "Think of the rock, so worn
With water, that when I gaze upon it I see
That I tremble too; I am confused as can be."

The wind picked up and together they embraced;
With love they were entwined and their blue hearts
Enlaced.

FRANCIS JAMMES

Is it the peculiar shape of the five curled hoods, which
look vaguely like the talon of an eagle (*aquila*), from
which the name of this flower, *Aquilegia* (columbine), was
derived? No one can say for sure.

Some draw a parallel between its Latin name, *Aquilegia*,
and *Aquilegium*, or water reservoir, claiming that the name
is derived from the volutes' capacity to collect dewdrops.
Still others maintain that the flower is called columbine
because the five tubular spurred petals of each flower look
like five doves (*columba*) drinking from a receptacle. It may
even be said that the petals are shaped like the fool's cap
worn during the Middle Ages, hence the flower's association with folly and extravagance.

Aquilegia

ANEMONE

■

Abandon

■

The bees in the anemone
Are begging in diligent swarms:
Spring offers them alms
In silver cups filled with money.

VICTOR HUGO

The fragile, ephemeral wild anemone is one of the earliest flowers to bloom in spring. It grows in the damp outskirts of the woods. Its colors range from white tinged with pink, magenta and mauve to deep blue.

Anemones, also called windflowers, are named after a young nymph with whom Zephyrus, the god of the west wind, fell in love. Zephyrus's wife was filled with jealousy and turned the Anemone into a flower so that her philandering husband could not have her. Anemones symbolize abandonment and waiting in anticipation.

The garden variety is sturdier, and its colors more violent, nearly tragic, ranging from brilliant crimson to deep violet blue. Tight bouquets of anemone buds sold in flower shops blossom and remain fresh in vases for long periods of time. The white crown wreathing the dark velvety center accentuates the lustrous blue, nearly black, stamen.

Anemone

ASPHODEL

■

Regret

■

O day that wanes in dreams
Dreams of her rising
From the folds of the dark lawn
And the red asphodel.

Asphodels grow tall and upright on the rocky hills surrounding the Mediterranean, where soil is sparse. The poet Francis Jammes described the flowers as "candles of the sun," given their tall height and the gleam of the white blossoms in sunlight.

They evoke the realm of Hades and the dead souls wandering through Elysian fields. One day, Persephone, the daughter of Zeus and Demeter, was seized with great admiration for a flower blowing gently in the breeze. When she reached down to pluck it, Hades split the earth and abducted her to be his queen in the Lower World. In light of this Greek myth, the asphodel is symbolic of regret, as well as immortality after death.

Asphodelus

HAWTHORN

■

Hope

■

Hawthorn, the dogrose and thyme
The carnation the lily and the rose
During this season sublime
Of the years bountiful prime
Their lavish robes unclose.

RÉMY BELLEAU

Before being Marcel Proust's *fleur-mémoire*, the hawthorn was the favorite flower of the great bards. How could the pastoral poets have resisted these bushes studded with white stars in all their rustic splendor? "The lovely hawthorn turning green" is like a wreath in the poems of Ronsard. In May in England, girls and boys frolicked in the woods and made wreaths of hawthorn; in the French countryside, children went from house to house gathering oboles and singing a beseeching song: "It's May, the lovely month of May," according to which wheat flourished and hawthorn bloomed "before God."

The hawthorn is the first awakening of nature and is symbolic of revival and hope as beautiful weather approaches.

Cratægus

WHEAT

Abundance
Wealth
Fertility

Before you vanish, pale
Star of the morning-time
— Myriad quail
Sing, sing amid the thyme
[...]
Turn your glance ere dawn's light
Drown it in blue defeat
— What delight
Fills the fields of ripe wheat!

PAUL VERLAINE

The staff of mankind, wheat is ground into flour, which is made into bread. The plant is highly symbolic of wealth, abundance, and fertility.

We recall the moral of the parable of the empty wheat sheaf standing upright and the sheaf heavy with grain drooping as a result of the weight: he who has no wealth seems pretentious, while he who has gained knowledge and life experience remains modest among his peers.

Triticum

BLUEBOTTLE

Delicacy
Purity of feelings

■

Gentle gatherer of the bluebottle
Who, in the meadow, under a clear sky
Wanders holding in her frail hand
A fresh bouquet of blue flowers.

AUGUSTE ANGELLIER

The bluebottle, which in the language of flowers means "delicacy" and purity of feelings, perhaps due to its fresh, pure color, is a very old flower that grows wild, notably in wheat fields.

Archeologists were surprised when they opened King Tutankhamen's tomb and found a simple bluebottle wreath still intact among the piles of gold accrued.

Several legends are associated with the flower. When a poisoned arrow wounded the centaur Chiron, the sap of the flower was used to heal his wounds. The flower has medicinal properties, and when steeped in hot water, it soothes the eyes. With the poppy, daisy, and wheat sheaf, the bluebottle forms a bright bouquet that is the symbol of France.

Centaurea Cyanus

HEATHER

∎

Solitude

∎

I plucked this sprig of heather;
Remember that autumn has passed
And we shall never meet again
The aroma of time, sprig of heather
Never forget how I await you.

GUILLAUME APOLLINAIRE

Heather blooms in the most remote areas—on deserted highlands, rocky hills, and steep rock formations, far from civilization. Its humble clusters quiver in the wind, and its pale pink bell-like flowers, which are nearly mauve-colored, evoke a feeling of muted sorrow, a resigned sense of self-effacement, yet delicate and moving at the same time. Heather is the mirror image of solitude.

Calluna Vulgaris

CAMELLIA

∎

White: Perfect beauty
Pink: Admiration
Red: Repentance

∎

I tended the garden
And then just after, the camellias
Fell.

SHIDA YAHA

The camellia originated in China and Japan, where it grows wild. It was introduced to Europe in the eighteenth century, and it flourished only by carefully shielding it from the cold. The mild climate of the Borromeo Islands on Lake Maggiore allowed the plant to flourish, and it is a true source of wonder to see the many varieties of the flower growing in clusters. Some are as white as wax, others a vibrant red or pink, still others striped in the most elaborate and imaginative patterns.

Alexandre Dumas *fils* made the flower the heroine of his novel *La Dame aux Camélias,* which inspired Verdi's opera *La Traviata.* The flower quickly became in vogue, with the white variety being worn on lapels. Coco Chanel played a major role in handing down the tradition.

Camellia Japonica

NASTURTIUM

Conquest

Patriotism

Treasure most the nasturtium, so joyful
In tones of aurora and flame.

HENRI POURRAT

The nasturtium is a distictive plant, with its handsome spurred flower. It was imported from Peru in the sixteenth century, but did not gain full recognition until two centuries later. Its exotic colors range from light yellow and orange to deep purple, contrasting sharply with the vivid blue-green foliage. The flat disk-shaped leaves run horizontally, bolstered by smooth upright stems. They look like miniature parasols. A pearly iridescent water drop gleams in the sunshine in the center of each leaf after a rainstorm.

The seeds are often pickled as capers and the tart buds and leaves are used in salads. There is no clear consensus as to the plant's actual taste, but the ornamental flowers are unequivocally lovely to look at. The nasturtium's bold shape and colors may be why it is associated with victory in battle and patriotism.

Tropæolum

THISTLE

∎

Agressivity

∎

I see the nettles and thistles
Hemlock and ocean bulrush
The trap and the tendon

And every plant that stabs and kills
Or who at all costs struggles.

EUSTACHE DESCHAMPS

The thistle is the national emblem of Scotland because during Malcolm I's reign in the fifteenth century, the Scottish army was rescued by the plant. As war was being waged against the Normans, one night, when the Scottish troops were asleep, the enemy decided to take them by surprise. The troops advanced silently but one of them stepped on a thistle and cursed so loudly that it woke up the Scots; they seized their weapons and waged a brilliantly successful battle.

Even the rugby uniforms of the Scottish team are emblazoned with the symbol of the thistle, the national emblem.

The motto of the Scottish Order of the Thistle, made up of sixteen aristocrats, is *"Nemo me impune lacesset"* (No one attacks me with impunity). In other words, "Whoever comes too close, gets pricked."

Cirsium Vulgare

OAK

■

Strength

Courage

Valor

■

Nestle to my breast your gentle leaves
O solitary oak!
Sow in my soul
Your passion so secret and tranquil.

FEDERICO GARCIA LORCA

The oak is the king of the forest, the most powerful of all trees. The Greeks believed that Zeus, the god of all gods, found refuge following his birth under the branches of an oak tree. The bards interpreted the murmuring of the leaves stirred by the wind and delivered their oracles. The Gauls also venerated the tree. Druids held ceremonies in the depths of the forest, and it is said that they cut off mistletoe with golden sickles. Schoolchildren learn that Saint Louis administered justice under an oak tree.

The oak symbolizes strength and courage, as well as valour; it crowned warriors. Gold-embroidered oak leaf trim is stitched on the caps of French generals.

Quercus Robur

H ONEYSUCKLE

Generous love
Attachment

The song of the honeysuckle

Of these two he was like
The honeysuckle
Attached to the hazel tree
Embracing and winding itself
Around the trunk that
Together they will forever endure
He who would unravel them
The hazel tree and the honeysuckle
They both would gladly kill.
Dear friend, and so are we
Neither me with you nor you without me.

MARIE DE FRANCE

The entwining shoots of the honeysuckle evoke the amorous embrace of true love. It is said that a honeysuckle plant sprang up from the tomb in which Heloise and Abelard were buried together. For some, the Latin *Caprifolium,* meaning "goat leaf," is close to the word "capriped," meaning "goat foot," and therefore feared by the superstitious.

Lonicera Caprifolium

CHRYSANTHEMUM

∎

Red: I love you
White: Truth
Yellow: Tenuous love

∎

Lively death my only season
White lilies, chrysanthemums
Bright nests devoid
Bruised leaves of April
Pleasant days gray with frost.

SAMUEL BECKETT

The chrysanthemum means "flower of gold" to the Greeks. It is true that the wild species bears only flowers that are bright yellow in color, but the Chinese and Koreans have grown a great variety of species for centuries—white, yellow, violet, gold, and rust in color.

The chrysanthemum is one of the favorite flowers of the Japanese, and festivals are held when they bloom. To the Japanese, the flower is symbolic of peace and strength of the soul in the face of adversity.

In France, the chrysanthemum blooms during the period of All Saint's Day and the Day of the Dead, and is thus placed on tombs.

The Japanese influence played a great role in the flower's popularity in Paris in the late-nineteenth- and early-twentieth-centuries. Marcel Proust's Odette de Crécy decorated her home with it. Today its association with death and mourning is waning, and is more frequently used in decorating homes.

Chrysanthemum

MEADOW SAFFRON

My best days are long gone

The meadow is poisonous but lovely in autumn
The cattle are grazing
Slowly poisoning themselves
The lilac and shadowy meadow saffron
Flowers here, your eyes resemble its bloom
Violet like the shadows and the autumn
And my life, slowly, with your eyes, is poisoned.

GUILLAUME APOLLINAIRE

The meadow saffron blooms in prairies and fields in fall. The plant is associated with a feeling of sadness and loss, as summer has waned and there is melancholy in the air. For Nature's cycle, the best days are long gone. Winter is nigh, when all flowers die.

In the countryside, the meadow saffron is sometimes called the nightlight: the oval cup formed by its petals contain bright orange stamens that look like tiny flames burning in an opaline cup, like a small light glowing by the deathbed.

Colchicum Autumnale

POPPY

∎

Sleep

Rest

Gratitude

∎

Dress these flowers of fire. They do not grow
In the woods, but in the fields of wheat, or rather
They grow the same in barren soil:
In the modest and simple garden of the gatekeeper.
They tremble when a train passes,
And trembling, die like those ardent of heart.

FRANCIS JAMMES

A Greek myth recounts how Persephone, Demeter's daughter, was abducted by Hades, god of the underworld. Demeter was crushed, but managed to persuade Zeus to allow her daughter to spend six months of the year on earth. Her return is marked by the flowering of poppies in the field.

The poppy belongs to the opium poppy family, but it effects are less powerful. It remains the symbol of sleep and oblivion to sorrow; however, the Greeks associate Morpheus, the god of sleep and dreams, with wreaths made of the red flowers.

Since the end of the Second World War, the English honor those who died in combat by wearing poppies in their lapels.

Papaver Rhoeas

DOGROSE

To the laden gloom of roses
Desire in the hands of the blind
Prefer, in passing, the dogrose
Of which I am the loving thorn
That survives your feelings of love.

RENÉ CHAR

In June, hedges and bushes are filled with the palest pink dogroses, or sweetbriars. Their arc-shaped stems and branches bend elegantly, with fragile petals scattered here and there. In autumn, the plants bear bright red fruit.

The dogrose is the flower of poets par excellence. The Academy of Floral Games, founded in 1323 in Toulouse, awarded the winners of poetry contests with a golden dogrose. Today, the *félibres*, members of a literary society of poets and prose writers formed in 1854 to preserve the Provençal dialect, wear this emblem on the lapels of their jackets.

Rosa Canina

Geranium

Geranium

Simplicity
Consolation

In an album
A fossil ghost
Geranium
Picked on the Coast

A Troubadour
Suave in ivory,
Mocks the flower
And her story...

"A requiem
Would please me well!"
"Nothing for you
Mademoiselle!"

Jules Laforgue

The geranium derives its name from the Greek *gerá-nion,* meaning "bill of the crane"; some species in the United States are cultivated in country gardens under the name cranesbill.

The bright hardy plants are easy to grow, making them ideal for balconies. They spruce up many towns and villages throughout Europe. The geranium symbolizes simplicity and consolation, given the plant's rusticity.

WALLFLOWER

∎

Fidelity in the face of adversity

∎

Simone, the sun smiles on the holly leaves
April has returned to play with us.

She scatters columbine and pansies
Hyacinth and the sweet scent of wallflowers.

REMY DE GOURMONT

The English named this flower after its characteristic trait of growing in the nooks and crannies of walls, quarries, and sea cliffs. It's hard to imagine a castle in Scotland without these yellow and orangish flowers shooting out of the old stones.

This is the sorrowful tale of the flower: In the land of ghosts in the thirteenth century, two young lovers were thwarted in that the maiden's father intended her to marry another. The young man was planning to kidnap her and she was to show her agreement by tossing him a wallflower growing out of the stone wall. Alas, however, she leaned too far out of the tower window and fell to her death at the foot of the tower. In great despair, the young man took the flower for his emblem: Loyalty in the face of adversity.

Cheiranthus Cheiri

GLADIOLA

∎

Provocation

∎

The wild gladiola, long-necked swan
And the divine laurel of exiled souls
Rosy like the seraphim's toe
Blushing with the lengthening dawn.

STÉPHANE MALLARMÉ

The shape of the long stiff pointed leaves influenced the symbolism of the gladiola. Its Latin name, gladiolus—so close in sound to gladiator—clearly indicates this and underscores the flower's seeming arrogance and combativeness.

The tall flowers can be arranged into striking bouquets and are ideal for decorating large sites. They are often placed on church altars or are given as prizes to champion athletes. Gladiola are frequently used in funeral ceremonies as well.

Gladiolus

Wistaria Sinensis

WISTERIA

Mutual trust
Cherished friendship

These waves of wisteria
Which I planted in my garden
To make a memory of you
When nostalgia wells up
Are now in bloom.

YAMABE NO AKAHITO

The purple drooping clusters of the most elegant member of the Papilionaceae family fall gently over arbors and walls. They symbolize mutual trust, as they cannot flourish alone, but must depend on the help of others. In exchange, the plants generously offers household thresholds, gateways, and pergolas magnificent streams of butterfly-like blossoms as part of the décor. The most beautiful varieties of wisteria were imported from China during the nineteenth century. Their highly decorative aspect of winding and twisting with drooping floral arcs inspired Art Nouveau artists. The wisteria's sweet pleasant fragrance inspired its name, *glykis* meaning "sweet" in Greek.

POMEGRANATE

■

Elegance
Pride
Ambition
Fertility

■

Beneath the window east of the Lady of Lu
Stands a pomegranate tree that is truly unique
The coral reflected by the green water
Cannot equal its brilliance.

LI PAI

It is believed that the pomegranate tree originated in Persia or Afghanistan. In Turkey during the sixteenth century an open pomegranate with the seeds exposed was often used in patterns in rich fabrics for caftans. The scarlet red color of the pomegranate tree flower resembles a proud flame.

The spherical, somewhat beveled fruit, which end in six points like a royal crown, and its dark, thick skin that gleams like Cordoba leather, is truly glorious to behold.

Cut into the rind and see the marvelous contents. The fruit is filled with translucid red seeds. The Provençal name for the pomegranate is *miograno* (a thousand seeds), which also makes it a symbol of fertility. The deep red jewel, the garnet, was named after the fruit, which is also called the pomegarnet.

A less poetic association—although more in tune with the arrogant plant itself—is the grenade and its associations with war.

Punica Granatum

GRASS AND HERBS

Purity
Consolation
Perseverance

■

I bring this evening my offering of joy
Having plunged myself in gold and silk
Of the frank and joyful wind and the sun so superb;
My feet are cleansed having walked through the
grass
My hands softened for having touched the heart
of flowers.

ÉMILE VERHAEREN

There are many allusions to grass in literature and poetry, or at least to "herbs", without specifying which species of the many plants grass and herbs entail.

Grass and herbs provide a wonderful emerald-colored showcase for wildflowers and lovers embracing. Their names remain obscure for the most part, except perhaps for crabgrass, which is the symbol of perseverance. The saying "to grow like crabgrass" is used in describing resistant plants that grow back again and again, despite the many attempts to eradicate them. Grass and herbs have many nicknames: one species of Lunaria is called "moonwort," after its full moon-like silicles which are filled with seeds and symbolize fertility. There is also agrimony or "herbe de Saint Guillaume," touted by Charlemagne in his Capitulaires; and hedge hyssop and Saint John's wort, with its renowned properties.

HOLLY

Srength

Eternity

Agressivity

∎

Oh bristled juniper, great desert lord!
And thorny holly, who in woods hold sway!
Ivy, the cavern tapestry! and gay
Bubbling streams that purl from sandy sward!
[...]
That I attend her grace though now downcast;
But if I must pursue this malady
I'd sooner die than languish to the last.

PIERRE DE RONSARD

The fact that this hardy bush remains green year round gives it an image of eternity. But the shape of its glossy spiny-toothed leaves, which are very sturdy and can cause pain if they come into contact with the body, associates the plant with aggression and combativeness.

Holly is a defensive plant which the druids used to ward off evil spirits. But holly with its bright red berries is strikingly beautiful, particularly in winter. Its festive appearance brightens homes at Christmas time, a time when flowers are difficult to obtain.

Ilex Aquifolium

IRIS

■

Good tidings

■

Drunkenness and sleep have untied
The knotted garlands of iris, ivy and fern
Which crowned his forehead with flickering shadows.

VIRGIL

The Iris originated in Syria. It was introduced to Egypt during the sixteenth century B.C. and was used for medicinal and magical purposes. The *Blue Bird Fresco* at Knossos in Crete depicts flowers that bear a close resemblance to the iris.

Iris was goddess of the rainbow and messenger of the gods in the *Iliad* and also in Virgil's work. This is why the flower is associated with tidings and good news.

The fleur-de-lis, which later became the emblem of French royalty was originally an iris. Louis VII, following a victory in a battlefield filled with yellow irises, chose the flower as his emblem. It was called "fleur-de-Louis," which later became fleur-de-lis.

During the Renaissance, Florentines steeped the gloves of ladies and gentlemen in a perfume derived from the root of the iris.

Iris

Iris

*Iris
Pseudacorus*

IRIS

The bitter-scented iris of blue, pale stemmed,
Slightly drooping, wilting, lonely in melancholy
Allows her long petals to hang.

LOUIS CHADOURNE

The Greeks called the rainbow "Iris's scarf," which was the pathway the goddess followed from the heavens down to earth.

HYACINTH

■

Red: Sorrow
Blue: Constancy
White: Discretion

■

I will plant white hyacinths
By my window, in the clear
Air, that will look like blue glass.

FRANCIS JAMMES

The young Hyacinth was loved by both Apollo and Zephyrus, god of the West Wind. One day, while they were playing discus, Zephyrus, who was jealous of Apollo, diverted the wind's course and caused Apollo to misdirect a discus throw, hitting the beautiful youth in the head and killing him. The hyacinth flower sprang from the earth where his blood fell.

Hyacinths come from western Asia. Turkish and Persian miniatures depict hyacinth sprigs bedecked in ribbons. The flower also appears in compositions featured in Persian fabrics and ceramic tiles.

The bulbs were introduced into Europe during the six-teenth century and a variety of species and colors were developed, each having its own meaning.

Endymion

JASMINE

Yellow: Grace, Elegance
White: Friendliness

Jasmine exudes a sweet scent
Flowers that the wind cannot stain
Whitest of white is your equal
Which you won't let me forget.

JEAN DE LA FONTAINE

This elegant plant originated in India. It is particularly loved for its heady fragrance and is used in a variety of designer perfumes.

The winding tendrils wrap around a variety of supports, creating elegant twists. An arbor filled with winding jasmine is a delight to the senses.

Tunisians make small bouquets of jasmine buds which children sell in open-air cafes and men sport tuck behind their ear.

Yellow jasmine, which is resistant to the cold, flowers in late winter when the earth is barren. Its yellow stars are the first stirring of nature.

Jasminum

LAUREL

∎

Glory
Victory

∎

I love the green laurel—neither winter nor frost
Can undo its victory in green
Revealing a forever happy eternity
That neither time nor death nor change can vanquish.

ÉTIENNE JODELLE

L aurel grows wild throughout the Mediterranean basin. The aromatic lance-like leaves of this evergreen shrub are used in cooking throughout the world. It is believed that the aroma of burnt laurel leaves inspired the pythia in Delphi as she delivered oracles.

Berry-bearing twigs of laurel were wound around the forehead of victorious heroes and poets in ancient Greece. The tradition was handed down and depicted in Renaissance sculpture and on coins. In France, during the nineteenth century, laurel wreaths were distributed along with awards in schools. The expression "to reap or win one's laurels" is derived from the plant, as is the laureate or winner.

Petrarch, when he lived in the Vaucluse, planted a laurel tree and wrote poems in its shade, said to be an homage to Laura de Noves, with whom he was in love.

Laurus Nobili

LAVENDER

■

Defiance

■

I awaited it, the pale gray lavender
Waited with all my heart its fragrant arrival
It came, I felt its scented touch
But it did not notice my eyes full of offering.

Marie Noël

The tradition that holds that lavender is the symbol of defiance is somewhat specious. Lavender, in fact, is a beneficent plant with renowned medicinal properties that is used as a disinfectant and a stimulant. It is grown in the Midi region of France, carpeting the landscape with a lovely deep purple. The plant adapts well to other climates; the English, for example, grow a great deal of lavender. Its fragrance is much sought after for use in soaps and eaux de toilette. Small brightly colored cloth bags are filled with the dried sheaves of the flower and used as sachets in cupboards and closets to freshen up linen and keep away mites.

In Provence, shepherds used to make lovely baskets using sprigs of lavender and narrow ribbons. This type of craftwork is making a comeback in women's boutiques.

Lavandula

IVY

Constancy
Eternal fidelity

■

The lush vines of ivy where shadows collect
Give rest to the evening as it sleeps in its leaves.

ANNA DE NOAILLES

Wild ivy creeps up tree trunks in the woods and along stone walls and arbors in gardens. Its small angled leaves and stems clinging by numerous radicated fibers are well anchored and are sometimes difficult to detach without breaking them. It is a symbol of eternal loyalty, its motto being "I Cling or I Die."

Ivy was sacred to Dionysus, who was depicted with a wreath of ivy, whose magical properties lured the Bacchantes. The great Greek poets were given ivy wreaths.

Creeping ivy entwined around young trees can kill them, perhaps representing overly possessive love.

Hedera Helix

LILAC

White: Innocence

Purple: First love

Come into the bower overhung with lilac
So that I might hold, so like a lozenge
Near your shoulder, the russet color of wheat
And smooth as the grape that sleeps on the wall,
A bengal rose dangling from a tendril.

FRANCIS JAMMES

The lilac originated in Persia, and was then introduced into Constantinople. Soon after, it reached France, where it grew wild.

The famous botanist Linnaeus named the flower *Syringa*, after the Greek word *syrinx,* meaning flute, perhaps due to its floral clusters that resemble champagne flutes. There are two varieties, purple and white. Both have an intensely fragrant aroma that is easy to identify from a distance as you stroll through the countryside.

During the nineteenth century, the flower was very much in vogue. Marcel Proust and other great authors alluded to the lilac, as did popular romances: "Come hither with me to celebrate spring, we'll gather lilacs and roses…"

Syringa vulgaris

Syringa Vulgaris

LILAC

▪

The day of the lilac and the day of the rose
Will never return to the days of this spring
The day of the lilac and the day of the rose
Have passed, the carnation too, this spring.

The winds have changed, the skies are morose
No longer we'll run, no longer gather
The flowing lilac and the beautiful rose
The spring is sad and no longer in bloom.

MAURICE BOUCHOR

This rather lackluster poem probably would have been relegated to oblivion if it hadn't so delightfully been set to music by Ernest Chausson in his *Poèmes de l'amour et de la mer.*

LILY

∎

Purity

∎

The poet claims that high among the stars
You climb each night to gather flowers
He claims he saw white Ophelia, floating on the
water
Like a giant lily, her long veils streaming.

ARTHUR RIMBAUD

The pristine white lily on its tall erect stem symbolizes purity.

Originally from Syria and Lebanon, the flower was brought to France by Crusaders; here, religious imagery associated the lily with the Virgin Mary. The symbol has endured to the present, and there are countless allusions to the lily in religious passages and imagery depicting wreaths of lilies surrounding the Virgin Mary and flowering lilies in her garden. In pictures of the annunciation, it is often placed in the hand of the archangel Gabriel.

The lily gives off a heady, sensuous aroma steeped in mystical meaning. Christ's teachings evoke the lily: "Consider the lilies of the field, how they grow; they toil not, neither do they spin: And yet I say unto you, That even Solomon in all his glory was not arrayed like one of these."

Lilium

BINDWEED

∎

Let us unite

∎

In the fields are the bindweeds
Glistening with dew—
A beautiful person
With lovely eyes.
I brought them together
And forever she's mine.

<small>CANON OF POEMS</small>

The fragile-looking wild bindweed raises its pale pink pavilions high, sometimes striped with a deeper-hued pink, entwining around stalks of wheat and grain. It is also a creeper, spreading over the ground. Bindweed mats or intertwines with plants among which it grows and is very difficult to remove once its braided twisting stems have entwined around an object, as it is highly resistant. "Let us unite"—or bind—is the flower's motto. Farmers see the plant as a nuisance, but its fresh blossoms are striking in their beauty.

Convolvulus Arvensis

Daisy

Innocence
Preference

■

I have forever inscribed in my heart
Above all others the daisy.
May it please God that one day
Intoxicated I may embrace it
And that love, this grace and favor shown me,
Shall let me in that season
Pluck this young russet flower
That only in growing bestows more beauty!
I shall ever have inscribed on my heart
The daisy above all other flowers.

JEAN DE LA TAILLE

The daisy represents innocence, given its sheer simplicity and whiteness. Children love to gather huge bouquets of daisies growing in fields.

The flower has another meaning, dating back to the Middle Ages: the knight who bore two daisies on his shield was the Lady's choice. If the Lady wore a crown of daisies, it meant that she still had not made up her mind.

The petals of the daisy are plucked one by one, leaving it up to pure chance to determine if "He loves me, he loves me not." Few may put stock in the ritual, but it is still an amusing little test.

Leucanthemum vulgare

Aesculus
Hippocastanum

CHESTNUT

■

Bravura
Dark melancholy

■

The flowers of the chestnut tree are already falling
It is snowing, snowing in May soft petals of pink.

ROSEMONDE GÉRARD

The horse chestnut migrated from India to Constantinople before reaching France in 1615, when three rootstocks were planted in Paris gardens.

Centuries have gone by, and the parks of Paris are now filled with horse chestnut trees, spreading their white- and pink-blossomed arms in spring and providing shade in summer. They once lined the boulevards and avenues of the city before the streets were widened for practical purposes.

In fall, the chestnut tree bears horse chestnuts. The spiny cases housing the fruit split and fall to the ground. They are called "Indian chestnuts," in honor of their provenance, and also to differentiate them from edible chestnuts. The Latin name, *hippocastaneus,* lies behind the name—horse chestnut.

MIMOSA

∎

Sensibility

∎

I came across a clump of great mimosas
They fell away from me as I passed through
They fell away with a subtle murmur
For these are the flowers of sensibility.

BLAISE CENDRARS

Did Blaise Cendrars speak the language of flowers? It is a strange coincidence that he unwittingly would attribute sensibility to the mimosa.

Mimosas grow in Africa and Asia and in tropical zones of Australia and America. They are perfectly acclimated to the Midi region of France, however, where they grow wild in the hills. They are sensitive to frost and need to be grown in greenhouses elsewhere.

Their downy pompons burst into bright yellow bloom in mid-February during Lent, when the flowers are used in celebrations. The floats used in carnivals and flower battles in Nice are decorated with mimosas.

Mimosa

LILY OF THE VALLEY

∎

Good luck

∎

When the new season arrives
When the frost has disappeared
We will go the two of us, my lovely
To gather the lilies in the woods.
Under our feet have fallen the flowers
That in the morning we saw trembling
We will go and listen to the blackbirds
Singing.

THÉOPHILE GAUTIER

The symbolism of the lily of the valley is widely understood even today. Every year on the first of May, people offer a sprig of this delicate flower, with its bright white bells and green wrapping, as a token of good luck.

Clusters of lily of the valley were often featured in Belle Époque post cards, with the tiny bells raised in relief to appear more lifelike.

The legend of the lily of the valley is religious in origin. Saint Leonard, a friend of Clovis, had withdrawn to the depths of the forest to live an ascetic life. One day, he was tempted by the devil, who assumed the form of a horrible dragon. The saint was wounded during the ferocious battle that ensued, and lily of the valley sprang up and blossomed from each drop of blood that fell to the ground. Lily of the valley is a lovely pleasantly scented flower, and you'll find it flourishing in the forest depths—although the dragons have disappeared.

Convallaria

MYOSOTIS

Forget me not

The blue flowered forget-me-not
Says to me: Do not forget
The dragonflies grazed me
With their tails during their frolicking.

THÉOPHILE GAUTIER

This lovely pale blue flower is so miniature and frail that it easily slips between the pages of a book or inside a folded letter. It conveys the message, "Be true to me." Its small blue face first surfaces on the edges of clearings and woods and the banks of streams in spring. It grows in virtually every herb garden.

The flower grows abundantly in Austria, where a legend is told about the flower. Two lovers were strolling along the banks of the Danube, when the young girl spotted a cluster of forget-me-nots floating on the water's surface. She had a great desire for the flowers and her lover, who sought to fulfill her every wish, went into the river to fetch the bouquet. Just as he handed her the bouquet, the river's powerful current swept him away. His last words were "Forget me not!"

Myosotis Sylvatica

MYRTLE

∎

Domestic bliss

∎

And my soul took flight
Pensive and softened,
To the myrtle grove where Virgil
Has made Dido the Phoenician
Wander for two thousands years.

FRÉDÉRIC PLESSIS

The Greeks honored Aphrodite with myrtle, and the Romans planted myrtle plants around the temple of Venus. The flower is symbolic of love. The plant originated in Asia and Africa and grows wild along the Mediterranean coast. The evergreen bush bears small white star-shaped flowers with light radiating stamens that give off a delicate bittersweet fragrance.

There are several legends from Antiquity associated with the flower, but the most beautiful one recounts how Aphrodite, as she came out of the sea naked, was pursued by satyrs and escaped their grasp by hiding in a copse of myrtle trees. The flower also symbolizes domestic bliss and was a traditional element in the wedding bouquet. Sometimes potted myrtle plants were given as wedding gifts to newly married couples. The myrtle was featured in Labîche's *Un Chapeau de Paille d'Italie.*

Myrtus

Narcissus

NARCISSUS

∎

Egotism
Self-love

∎

The petrifying water kills
No one. Dive in, Narcissus.
Let us hope that you succeed
In becoming your own statue.

JEAN COCTEAU

The slightly flat stem of the narcissus stands steadfast and erect, bearing a small cone of rumpled paper with a white flower and reddish rim on the corona. The jonquil is yellow in color, with a trumpet-shaped center that is deeper yellow. The heady, almost intoxicating fragrance of the narcissus fills the fields in spring.

In *Metamorphoses*, Ovid depicts Narcissus as a beautiful youth who fired the heart of nymphs, particularly that of his cousin Echo. Narcissus spurned all offers of love, loving only himself. Echo pined away until nothing was left of her but her voice. One day, he became enamoured of his own reflection in a pool of water. To punish him, Cupid turned him into a flower.

The Freudian term narcissism, inspired by the Greek myth, describes someone who is totally self-absorbed.

WATER LILY

∎

Coldness
Purity of heart

∎

On the soft and mottled banks by the spring
The petals hang from the golden lilies
And there in the fields and orchards
Can be heard its distant echo in the shepherd's song.

THÉODORE DE BANVILLE

The name of the water lily, of the genera *Nymphea*, is derived from the Greekword *nymphe*, any of a large number of minor female deities associated with trees or water and represented as beautiful, eternally young virgins. Their virginity is undoubtedly the origin of the flower's association with coldness.

Pond lilies bear round yellow showy flowers that bloom on the surface of slow-moving water and are rooted in the bed by long trailing stems. Water lilies, from the same family but with larger white blossoms slightly tinted purple, float on still water. Another variety is the lotus, which open in the morning and closes at night. The lotus is sacred to the Egyptians and is a traditional motif in Egyptian art and architecture.

Claude Monet diverted a stream at Giverny to build a pond, where he planted water lilies, which inspired his magnificent series of paintings.

Nymphea

CARNATION

◼

Red: Passion

Heartbreak

Freedom

◼

Bushy clumps, the green branches entwine
The red flowers hang like bursts of light
I always fear that the dew will not fall
And that the flower will not live out their destinies.

WANG-TSI

The fiery red carnation symbolizes passionate love, yet the pain of heartbreak. Its spicy, subtle fragrance matches the capricious shape of its serrated petals. Linnaeus named the genus *Dianthus,* flower of the gods.

The flower is featured in many Renaissance poems, as is the rose and the lily. Many paintings and illuminated manuscripts feature the carnation, and the flower is used in religious imagery. The red carnation has become symbolic with freedom, which reached an apotheosis during the "Carnation Revolution" in Portugal. Nice and the Italian Riviera are major carnation-growing areas, and long greenhouses, which shelter the flowers during the winter, line the hillsides and overlook the sea. The carnation has many different meanings, depending on the variety and color.

Dianthus Caryophyllus

Dia

CARNATION

Red carnation: Passion
White carnation: Talent
Striated carnation: Refusal
Yellow carnation: Disdain
Sweet William: Desire to please
Garden pink: Grace

In the scented garden of herbs and carnations
When dawn has wetted the tufted
wild thyme
And the heavy hornets hovering above the
tomatoes
Totter while laden with pollen and dew,

I will come at daybreak in the mist of the morn
Heady with the season and the
burgeoning day
My heart will swell like the
cock that crows
Incessantly at the
rising of the sun.

ANNA DE NOAILLES

OLIVE TREE

Wisdom
Peace

Do you know it, Daphne, that ancient romance
At the foot of the sycamore or beneath the white laurel
Under the olive tree, the myrtle or the weeping willow
This song of love that always begins anew.

GÉRARD DE NERVAL

The silvery-leafed olive tree is indestructible; when cut or burned, it grow back eternally. The tree was sacred to the ancient Greeks, who crowned their heroes and Olympic athletes with olive branches. Poseidon, the god of the sea, and Athena, the goddess of wisdom, were asked to choose a name for the largest city in Greece, but they were unable to reach a decision. Poseidon struck the ground with his trident and a spirited stallion—a symbol of war— sprang up. Athena in turn made an olive tree—symbol of peace—spring up from the ground. Zeus chose her offering and the city was christened Athens.

The olive supplies oil, which is a staple ingredient in ancient Greek and Roman cuisine. Throughout the Mediterranean basin where the olive tree flourishes, it is still a major ingredient in many dishes today.

Olea Europea

ORANGE TREE

Virginity

Take, my dear, this orange
I give it to you out of love
Do not cut it with a knife
For my heart rests inside

CANTES FLAMENCOS

The orange tree, inextricably associated with the gardens at Alhambra and the fragrant aroma of Andalusian orange groves, bears buds, flowers, and fruits at the same time. Originally from India, the tree easily was acclimated throughout the Mediterranean basin. The golden fruit has not always been such a common commodity, however. In the Middle Ages, oranges were given as valuable gifts, and until the end of the nineteenth century, children saw oranges as a delightful treat.

The buds of orange blossoms are hidden underneath the glossy bright green leaves. Orange blossoms symbolize virginity and were used to crown the bridal veil or in the wedding bouquet. The wedding crown traditionally was kept in a glass bowl in the newlyweds' bedroom for as long as they lived. They can still be found in various antique shops.

Citrus Aurantium

ORCHID

∎

Supreme beauty

Luxury

∎

In the morning I pick orchids in the garden
Fearful they may perish in the frost
In the evening, as storm clouds gather,
I return to my lair, where,
On the rocks, I amuse myself with the moon.

SIE LING-YUN

Orchids grow spontaneously in Europe, including members of the spotted, speckled, mottled, and flecked *Orchis*, and of *Ophrys*, spurless orchids with convex lips suggesting the body of an insect, hence the common names bee-orchis, spider-orchis, as well as others. They are strange, intensely rich, elegant flowers that are quite odd at times, even frightening. Their aroma is subtle yet insidious. Unfortunately, many species of orchid are endangered and are now protected.

In the eighteenth and nineteenth centuries, explorers brought back other sumptuous species to Europe. William Cattley invented a new form of orchid growing, which produced the Cattleya orchid, so frequently featured in Proust's works. The flowers were so widely admired that an illustrated magazine with botanical images was launched and published for sixteen years. The original plates are housed at the Museum of Natural History in London.

Orchis
Morio

Bellis Perennis

ENGLISH DAISY

Innocence

The grass explodes with daisies
The scents we think are silent
Count the secret sorrows
Of the bindweeds and bluebottles.

The little white wings
On the water and furrows
Tumble in cascades;
A blizzard of butterflies.

VICTOR HUGO

The English daisy is the daisy's little sister, with a similar crown of narrow petals encircling a yellow raised heart. Each petal is tipped with the slightest tinge of bright pink.

They grow in clumps of roundish leaves that are velvety green. The tight, round buds give just the slightest hint of the beauty that is soon to burst forth.

The English daisy flowers at Easter time, heralding spring, as well as in autumn when the climate is mild. They decorate lawns in parks, and are favorites with children, who transform them in tiny bouquets for their mothers.

The Renaissance poets were drawn to the flower's sheer simplicity, and they paid tribute to it endlessly.

PASSIFLORA

∎

Mystical passion

∎

Mystical passion
The blue passiflora
The butterflies anvil
Do you thrive in the mire of time?
[...]
Clear blue star
The aurora's navel
Do you thrive in the froth
Of the shade?

FEDERICO GARCIA LORCA

The passiflora, or passionflower, is originally from North America. Those seen by early Spanish settlers were interpreted as symbolic of the Crucifixion, with the ten petals and sepals, fringed corona, five stamens, three styles, and coiling tendrils representing respectively the ten faithful apostles, the crown of thorns, wounds, nails, and scourges. The religious symbols featured widely on missals.

The large-fruited granadillas, with the egg-shaped fruits being either yellow or orange in color, enclose red seeds that look like drops of dried blood. Some of the fruits are edible.

Passiflora
Caerulea

OPIUM POPPY

∎

Sleep
Death

∎

Sleep has touched her eyes;
Under succulent opium poppies
They close, and her heart stands by.

ÉVARISTE PARNY

The Latin name for the opium poppy is *Papaver somni-ferum*—or sleep-inducer. It looks very much like the poppy, although it is larger and more majestic. The flowers can be white, pink, or red.

The medicinal poppy contains a bitter milky substance that is extracted from the capsule. This is opium, which has played a major role in the Orient. The green parts of the plant are poisonous. They contain morphine and codeine. Only the tiny bluish seeds are harmless.

The Romans made pastries by mixing poppy seeds with honey, which were considered a delicacy. Today they are sprinkled on breads, rolls and cookies.

Until the seventeenth century, poppies were used in China for opium; in Europe, they were used strictly for medicinal purposes to allay pain. Today, however, an increase in travel and exchanges have seen a rise in the use of the drug in the West, giving rise to an immensely lucrative trade. More and more of the flower is being planted. The plant symbolizes sleep and is associated with death.

Papaver Somniferum

PANSY

∎

Remembrance

∎

Purple flowers of velvet so suffering
From your soft eyes the color of pansies.

JOHN ANTOINE NAU

The pansy, whose Latin name is *Viola tricolor,* is a species of violet. It is much larger than the violet, however, and its petals come in a variety of deep velvety colors: white, violet, yellow, and pale blue. According to the language of flowers, the attributed meanings of pansy are pleasant thoughts; modesty; and think of me.

This is why Ophelia included pansies in the bouquet of flowers she gave her brother before dying: think of me.

In *A Midsummer Night's Dream,* Shakespeare, who was well-versed in the language of flowers, asks Puck to gather pansies, also called love-in-idleness, and to moisten Tatiana's eyelids with their extract so that she would fall in love with the first man she sees after awakening.

The pansy featured very frequently in religious imagery in the late-nineteenth- and early-twentieth-centuries, as well as in postcards, illustrated with pansies and lovely ladies, saying "With thoughts of you."

Viola

PERIWINKLE

Fidelity in friendship

As in times gone by, the periwinkle
On the soft velvety green of the meadow
In the mottled time of spring
Hangs its heavenly blue chalice of nectar
Upon the sun's supple rays.

THÉOPHILE GAUTHIER

The *Vinca Major,* a perennial with evergreen glossy leaves, grow in shaded woods in France, while *Vinca Minor,* which has smaller flowers, flourishes in drier soil. They are trailing shrubs with opposing leaves.

Some of the common names for the flowers—"shepherd," "wee virginity," and "witches' violet" (it was believed to be a key ingredient used in witches' brews), among others—are quite amusing. The heavenly blue color of the flowers evoke images of "baby blue eyes." The flower symbolizes fidelity in friendship.

Well after his separation with Madame de Warens, Jean-Jacques Rousseau, who was gathering wild herbs in the woods, discovered a periwinkle. In his beautiful work *Confessions,* he described the rush of warm memories that came back every time he thought of this flower, which made him think of Madame de Warens. Rousseau had come up with his own remembrance of things past—that Proustian rush triggered by the sight of a madeleine—well before Marcel Proust himself did.

Vinca Major

Vinca Major

PEONY

Bashfulness

A bee escapes
From the heart of a peony
With such regret!

MATSUO BASHO

The peony, or *Paeonia,* was named after Peon, a doctor to the Greek gods. He cured Hades, the god of the underworld, when he was ill, using herbal tea made from peony seeds. The legend spread, and the plant was seen as having medicinal properties in the Middle Ages, which is why it was grown in medicinal herb gardens in monasteries. The actual medical properties have never been confirmed, however.

The peony is a symbol of shyness. Chinese poetry has frequently used the flower as a metaphor for a blushing young girl. The French have an expression that goes "as red as a peony."

The Chinese and Japanese are particularly fond of the peony and excel in its cultivation. Artists frequently feature the flower in silk paintings and prints.

Paeonia Officinalis

Paeonia

APPLE TREE

∎

Flower: Repentance
Fruit: Temptation
Disobedience

∎

You never again knew the tree laden with apples
Bending with the burden of ripeness
You never again knew before your house
The young wheat sprout forth for the joy of our
children.

CHARLES PÉGUY

The meaning of the apple tree differs if it refers to the fruit as opposed to the flower. The apple has taken on greater symbolism than the flower has, notably because of two magnificent gardens.

The Garden of the Hesperides is where the Hesperides guarded the tree bearing the golden apples given by Gaea to Hera when she married Zeus. One of the labors of Heracles was to slay the seven-headed dragon guarding the golden apples and carry them off. A golden apple inscribed with "To the most beautiful" was claimed by Hera, Athena, and Aphrodite and was the source of a great dispute. This is the origin of the expression "apple of discord."

The second garden is the Garden of Eden, where Satan tempted Adam and Eve to taste the forbidden fruit of the Tree of the Knowledge of Good and Evil, thus unleashing sin upon the world.

Pyrus Malus

COWSLIP

Candor

Hidden by a cowslip,
A quail, a warbling blackbird,
Drank together from the same cup
In a belladonna in bloom.

VICTOR HUGO

In March and April, just as the snow is beginning to melt, bright yellow clumps of cowslip begin to appear. The fresh, simple flowers spring up from long, pale, embossed leaves with a velvety underlining. The flower heralds spring, and in Italian is called *primavera*—literally meaning "spring."

According to a German legend, souls seeking to enter the kingdom of Heaven tried to slip in through a small side door, Saint Peter having locked the gates. Saint Peter was distracted and dropped the keys, which took root and turned into clumps of cowslips. This is why the flowers are also called "tiny keys to heaven."

Primula veris

Rosmarinus Efficinalis

ROSEMARY

∎

Memory

∎

If you want me to love you
Adorn yourself with the scent of rosemary
To chase away the odors
Of all previous lovers.

CANTES FLAMENCOS

Rosemary, derived from the Latin for "dew of the sea," is an stiff shrub that grows on limestone hillsides and slopes, particularly by the seaside. The bushy shrub has narrow opposing pungent leaves and usually bears delicate light blue or white flowers at the end of winter.

Its characteristic aroma makes it an ideal herb to accompany mutton and lamb. The branches can be used to fashion rustic shish kebabs by sharpening the ends and skewering the meat. This technique brings the fragrant leaves in contact with the inner flesh of the meat, adding a delicious flavor.

The queen of Hungary claimed that rosemary added to water rejuvenated her and that her gout was cured by applying the precious liquid. Rosemary is associated with memory and mourning and is often planted near tombs. In Spain, the floors of churches are strewn with rosemary during Holy Week.

BRAMBLES

Sorrow

Difficulty

■

The house is so fresh in the midst of the sun,
As if it had bathed.
The brambles are wet from the rainbow
Like heavy spiderwebs.

FRANCIS JAMMES

A member of the Rosaceae family, brambles grow in ruins, wastelands, and enclosed areas. They bear lovely tiny pink flowers and produce tasty berries, but they are more notorious for their thorns.

Religious imagery depicts the bramble as a symbol of the difficulties of life on earth, the "path strewn with brambles and thorns," which is the lot of humanity. The plant is associated with the tragic events of the Passion of Jesus Christ, whose head was crowned with thorns.

Rubus Fructicosa

ROSE

∎

White and red: Love
Passion

∎

When I saw the rose over the thorn
I felt by its petals cast in the shade
The rose from its color at evening is torn
The other from its color never will fade.

PIERRE DE RONSARD.

The rose is the queen of all flowers, and has been a part
of virtually every civilization for over three thousand
years. According to one legend, Sargon, the king of
Sumer, introduced the rose into the capital. The flower
decorated the famous Gardens of Babylon. The Chinese
have been growing roses since ancient times. The Persian
poet Sadi praised the rose in his famous *Gulistan* or
Garden of Roses, and the flower is depicted in the *Bluebird
Fresco* at Knossos in Crete.

In Rome, the rose was part of celebrations and festivities, as well as orgies. Rose petals were mixed with wine
and showered over guests. The ground was strewn with
them, and rose petals were used to perfume bath water.
The Renaissance poets, adapting ancient traditions, featured the rose as a favorite flower: "O dearest, let us go
and see if the rose…"

Rosa

ROSE

■

■

I see in the rose a half-open book
Of countless pages
Of intricate joys
That we will never read.

RAINER MARIA RILKE.

You who, without letting fall your petals,
Without dying, will succumb
O rose forever fresh in the roughest of winds.

GUILLAUME APOLLINAIRE

ROSE

The roses of Saadi

I wanted to bring you some roses this morning;
But I had wrapped so many into my sash
So tight were the knots it could not hold them.

The knots broke. The roses were scattered
In the wind until they reached the sea.
They followed the water to never return.

Until the waves were red and seemed aflame:
This evening, my robe is still steeped in their scent
Inhale then the aroma of remembrance.

MARCELINE DESBORDES-VALMORE

Rosa

YELLOW ROSE

Infidelity

I love, o cuddly wolf, the whimpering of your voice.
I love its coarse and undulating tone, but I also love
Above all, I love to death your nose, your
Little nose that just escapes your locks
Like a yellow rose hidden in dark foliage.

JORIS-KARL HUYSMANS

During the Middle Ages, the secular meaning of the rose was overshadowed by its religious meaning. "The mystical Rose" became the spiritual embodiment of the Virgin Mary. The rose has been featured in countless paintings and retables with figures from the Marial cult.

Not long ago, rose petals were strewn by children along the pathways of processions. You can find rosaries with scented beads made from compressed rose petals at the charterhouse of Granada in Spain. On a more frivolous note, single roses, rose scrolls, bouquets of roses in full flower, or rosebuds were a very common theme for decorating silks and percales, and for embroidered patterns on dresses and vests during Louis XV's reign.

In the early-nineteenth-century, Pierre-Joseph Redouté represented roses with a nearly magical perfection.

Roses today are produced according to highly scientific methods, with new species being created for a booming international market.

Rosa

HOLLYHOCK

Fertility

A tall hollyhock
Composed on a thistle-clad roof
Its bells full of light
Where rang out the bumblebees.

VICTOR HUGO

The hollyhock, or "holy hock," can grow as tall as seven feet. With its vertical stance, it was once a symbol of majestic beauty. Its large single or double flowers are scattered up and down the entire stalk and can be white, light yellow, pink, red, or purple. A feathery protuberance covered in pollen draws many insects.

When the flower wilts, it gives way to a kind of circular disk enclosing hundreds of seeds neatly arrayed in a radiating pattern. Their sheer number lies behind the hollyhock's association with fertility.

The hollyhock grows primarily in impoverished soil. They are not used in bouquets, although Flemish painters depicted them in their compositions, and they appeared in Art Nouveau wallpaper and fabrics. They provide a flamboyant décor on house facades and form a kind of floral fence on the outskirts of gardens.

Althea Rosea

SAGE

Strength

Health

■

Whoever grows sage
In his garden
Has no need
For a doctor.

POPULAR SAYING

Sage is one of the humblest of flowers, but it has many virtues. It is easy to grow, requiring little pruning or fertilizing. In Provence, sage flourishes in dry or gravely soil. Its name, Salvia, is derived from the word *salvare,* to save, hence its reputation for guaranteeing good health.

Popular tradition recommends steeping the plant as a remedy for a wide variety of ailments. Although this remains to be proven, it is certain that the herbal tea is delicious. Sage is also used in cooking to flavor pork, game and cold cuts.

One legend recounts how during the flight from Egypt, the Virgin hid baby Jesus in sage. Grateful, she granted the plant medicinal properties, which is why it became associated with salvation.

Salvia Officinalis

MARIGOLD

Chagrin

You gather in your basket
Like a flower among seated flowers
The color of yellow, incarnate and gray
Sometimes russet and white, and also
Red carnation, the yellowing marigold.

PIERRE DE RONSARD

The yellow and orange petals of the marigold radiate like little suns. The origin of its name *Solsequium*—he who follows the sun—illustrates the flower's relation to the heavenly body. Wild marigolds open with the first rays of sunshine and close in late afternoon. Like so many other flowers, the marigold has its own particular hour on nature's clock.

Its yellow color, traditionally seen as a negative shade, has given the flower a variety of negative meanings: jealousy, chagrin, and torment. It is rare to offer a bouquet of marigolds, although the language of flowers reveals that meanings can be tempered by including other more positive flowers along with it.

Flower markets often have floral compositions which include the marigold with other flowers. Centuries ago, the flower's symbolism was more positive. Ronsard wrote vivid verses about the flower, using the earlier name of cockscomb and yellow marigold.

Calendula

Trifolium

CLOVER

White: Think of me
Red: Dedication
Four-leaf clover: Good luck

You smell like clover,
You smell like milk, fennel and aniseed.
You smell like nuts, you smell like berries
Which are well ripened for us to pluck.

REMY DE GOURMONT

Clover is a common perennial, with three leaves, round or pointed, and flowers like white, pink, or rosy pom-poms. It is a fodder crop that grows in cool, damp areas and would probably be ignored by many if it weren't for—by some freak of nature—the four-leaf clover. The four-leaf clover is extremely rare, as it is a freak of nature. People spend long hours looking for them, but often the effort is futile. Anyone who finds one, how-ever, is thrilled, given that the plant means good luck. They are used to make small jewelry, bracelets, and brooches that are worn to conjure this luck that accompanies the plant.

TULIP

Red: Declaration of love
Yellow: Hopeless love
Reknown

My friends, spring is sprung, the roses unfold
Spring is all a fire, the tulip smiles
On the face of love, the flowerbed in bloom
It is the season of light and the tulip nods.

NEDIM

The tulip originated in the East and has been a favorite motif for Persian fabrics and ceramics.

The word "tulip" may have been derived from the Turkish *tolipend,* or "turban," perhaps in reference to the multi-colored turbans of Ottoman troops streaming across the fields to battle like bright tulips. In the eighteenth century, Oriental gardens were planted with tulips, and miniatures depicted them in great detail.

The Venetians introduced the tulip into Holland in the mid-sixteenth-century, and a tulip-mania soon broke out. It was a favorite flower of the Dutch painters, as any visit to one of the Netherlands' museums reveals. A great variety of species were developed, notably the striated tulip.

Soon all of Europe was hit with this tulip-mania, particularly in France. In Caractères, La Bruyère described the "tulip lover," a collector willing to go to rack and ruin to obtain a bulb of the latest tulip species. Tulips are frequently given as gifts, despite the drawback that the flower has virtually no scent.

Tulipa

GRAPEVINE

∎

Drunkeness

∎

On the old bench overshadowed with vines
Clydia with vestal snood, swan-necked Clydia
Unwinds, to embroider birds and flowers,
A silken skein of brilliant colors.

ALBERT SAMAIN

The grapevine is most closely associated with Dionysus, known as Bacchus to the Romans, who is depicted crowned with vine leaves and holding a goblet. The god of wine and intoxication lorded over all celebrations and frenzied festivities, accompanied by satyrs, Sileni and Bacchantes, which inevitably ended in orgies. Literary contests were held during the rites of initiation, and Dionysus also became associated with poetry and music.

According to the Romans, Bacchus came across a grapevine that was so tiny and frail that he implanted the bone of a bird to protect the plant and help it grow. As the vine flourished, the bone became that of a lion, then that of an ass. The moral of the story is whoever drinks wine becomes as merry as a lark, then as strong as a lion, and ultimately as foolish as an ass.

vitis vinifera

VIOLET

■

Modesty

Decency

■

The forward violet thus I did chide:
Sweet thief, whence didst thou stesl my sweet that
smells,
If not from my love's breath? The purple pride
Which on thy soft cheek for complexion dwells
In my love's veins thou hast too grossly dyed.

WILLIAM SHAKESPEARE

The delicate violet flourishes in gardens and woods, its erect stem drooping slightly at the top, as if bending its head toward the ground. This is perhaps why the flower is associated with modesty and decency.

The flower, a favorite during Antiquity, was featured in Petrarch's poems and scattered throughout Shakespeare's works. Round bouquets of violets, with the flowers nestling in a girdle of downy bright green leaves, added a chic touch to Belle Époque attire. Violets frequently are sold on street corners in late winter. Cultivated violets are larger and have double flowers. They are a specialty of Parma, Italy, as well as Toulouse, France. The cultivated species are like aristocrats in comparison to the humble wild violets. But wild violets are intensely more fragrant than the richer, more "tailored" ones.

Viola Odorata

Symbols and Flowers

Flowers and Symbols

Sources

Yamabe NO AKAHITO p. 49: excerpt from *Poèmes d'amour*. Poésie Gallimard.

Auguste ANGELLIER p. 20: "Ma Cueilleuse de bleuets" in *Le Chemin des saisons*. Éditions Archipel.

Anonymous (11th–6th cent. B.C.) p. 76: excerpt from *Canon des poèmes*. *Anthologie de la poésie chinoise classique*. Gallimard.

Guillaume APOLLINAIRE p. 22: "L'Adieu," p. 36: excerpt from "Les Colchiques," in *Alcools*. P. 128: excerpt from *Poèmes à Lou*.

Théodore de BANVILLE p. 92: excerpt from "Allons voir le matin se lever" in *Poésies*. Fasquelle.

Matsuo BASHO p. 114: in *Anthologie de la poésie japonaise classique*. Poésie Gallimard.

Samuel BECKETT p. 34: excerpt from *Poèmes*. Éditions de Minuit.

Rémy BELLEAU p. 16: excerpt from "Avril" in *La Nature. Première journée de la bergerie*. Éditions Jacques Petit.

Maurice BOUCHOR p. 73: excerpt from "Le Temps des lilas" in *Poèmes de l'amour et de la mer. Chagrins d'amour*. Le Cherche-Midi Éditeur.

René CHAR p. 40: from "The Clear Seeing," Bloodaxe Books, 1992).

Louis CHARDOUNE p. 59: excerpt from "Jardins de novembre" in *Accords*. Gallimard.

Blaise CENDRARS p. 82: excerpt from "Vomito negro" in *Le Sud*. Denoël.

Jean COCTEAU p. 91: "Vase avec anse" in *Faire part*. Poésie club, librairie Saint-Germain-des-Prés.

Marcelline DESBORDES-VALMORE p. 128: "Les Roses de Saadi" in *Poésies posthumes*.

Eustache DESCHAMPS p. 28: excerpt from "Ballade des mauvaises herbes."

Marie de FRANCE p. 32: "Lai du chèvre-feuille."

Federico GARCIA LORCA p. 30: excerpt from "Chêne," p. 106: excerpt from "Interrogations," in *1921–1922, Livre de poèmes, Suites et Premières Chansons*. Poésie Gallimard.

Théophile GAUTIER p. 84: excerpt from "Villanelle," p. 86: excerpt from "La Source," p. 112: excerpt from "Élégie" in *Poésies complètes*. Fasquelle.

Rosemonde GÉRARD p. 81: excerpt from "Les Marronniers" in *Les Pipeaux*.

Remy de GOURMONT p. 44: excerpt from "Avril," p. 139: excerpt from "Les Cheveux" in *Divertissements*. Mercure de France.

Fujiwara NO HIROTSUGU p. 8: in *Anthologie de la poésie japonaise classique*. Poésie Gallimard.

Victor HUGO pp. 12, 132: excerpt from "L'Église," p. 118: excerpt from "La Primevère," in *Chanson des rues et des bois*. P. 105: "Juin" in *Les Contemplations*.

Joris-Karl HUYSMANS p. 130: excerpt from "Rococo japonais" in *Le Drageoir aux épices. Anthologie des poètes délaissés*. La Table Ronde.

Francis JAMMES pp. 10, 70: excerpt from "Tristesses," pp. 38, 122: excerpt from "Le Poète et sa femme," in *Clairières dans le ciel*. Gallimard. P. 60: excerpt from "Je mettrai" in *De l'angelus de l'aube à l'angelus du soir*. Mercure de France.

Étienne JODELLE p. 64: extrait de "Sonnet" in *Amours. Anthologie des poètes délaissés*. La Table Ronde.

Jean de LA FONTAINE p. 62: excerpt from "L'Orangerie" in *Les Amours de Psyché*.

Jules LAFORGUE p. 43: from "Rigors Like None Other."

Jean de La TAILLE p. 78: excerpt from "Le Blason de Marguerite" in *Les Fleurs dans la poésie française*. Plon.

Guy LEVIS MANO pp. 100, 121: excerpt from *Cantes flamencos*. Club français du livre.

Sie LING-YUN p. 102: "La Nuitée sur l'escarpement de Che-Men" in *Anthologie de la poésie chinoise classique*. Gallimard.

Stéphane MALLARMÉ p. 46: excerpt from "Les Fleurs" in *Poésies*. Éditions Deman.

John-Antoine NAU p. 110: excerpt from "Sur l'arc vert de la plage apaisée" in *Les Hiers bleus*. Éditions Meissen.

NEDIM p. 140: excerpt from "Chanson" in *Anthologie de la poésie turque*. Gallimard.

Gérard de NERVAL p. 98: excerpt from "Delfica" in *Les Chimères*.

Anna de NOAILLES p. 68, p. 97: excerpt from "Le Jardin et la maison" in *Le Cœur innombrable*.

Marie NOËL p. 66: excerpt from "Chanson" in *Les Chansons et les heures*. Stock.

LI PAI p. 50: "Le Grenadier de la fenêtre est de la voisine" in *Poésie chinoise*. Marabout université.

Evariste PARNY p. 108: excerpt from "Le Songe" in *Poésies érotiques. Anthologie des poètes délaissés*. La Table Ronde.

Charles PÉGUY p. 116: excerpt from "Début D'Ève" in *Prières*. Plon.

Frédéric PLESSIS p. 88: excerpt from "Arbor infelix" in *La Lampe d'argile. Chagrin d'amour*. Le Cherche-Midi Éditeur.

Henri POURRAT p. 26: excerpt from "Le Jardin" in *Almanach des quatre saisons*. Albin Michel.

Arthur RIMBAUD p. 74: excerpt from "Ophélie" in *Œuvres complètes*. La Pléiade, Gallimard.

Rainer Maria RILKE p. 126: excerpt from *Les Roses, II. Anthologie des poètes délaissés*. La Table Ronde.

Pierre de RONSARD p. 54: extrait du Sonnet XLIV in *Sonnets pour Hélène*. P. 124: excerpt from "Chanson" in *Les Amours de Marie*. P. 136: excerpt from l'Élégie XX.

Albert SAMAIN p. 142: excerpt from "Clydie" in *Le Chariot d'or*. Mercure de France.

William SHAKESPEARE p. 144: excerpt from Sonnet XCIX in *Sonnets*.

Paul-Jean TOULET p. 14: excerpt from *Contrerimes*, in *Chagrin d'amour*. Le Cherche-Midi Éditeur.

Émile VERHAEREN p. 52: excerpt from "Les Heures" in *Les Heures d'après-midi*. Mercure de France.

Paul VERLAINE p. 18: excerpt from "Aurore" in *La Bonne Chanson*.

VIRGILE p. 56: excerpt from l'Eglogue VI des *Bucoliques*.

Shida YAHA p. 24: in *Anthologie de la poésie japonaise classique*. Poésie Gallimard.

WANG-TSI p. 94: excerpt from "L'Œillet" in *Anthologie de la poésie chinoise classique*. Poésie Gallimard.

All translations from French texts are by John Herrick, unless otherwise specified.

Bibliography

Arzik, Nimet. *Anthologie de la poésie turque du XIIIe au XXe siècle*, Connaissance de l'Orient, Gallimard, 1994
Frain, Irène. *La Guirlande de Julie*. Robert-Laffont, 1991
Goody, Jack. *La Culture des fleurs*. Seuil, 1994
Groult, Flora. *"Voici des roses," Poésies choisies*. Archipel, 1994
Guy Levis Mano. *Cantes Flamencos*. Club français du livre
Maynial. *Anthologie des poètes du XIXe siècle*. Hachette, 1952
Pickles, Sheila. *Le Langage des fleurs du temps jadis*. Solar, 1994
Redouté, P.-J. *Les Roses*. Bibliophilie pour tous.
Schnitzer, Rita. *Légende des fleurs*. Éditions du Chêne, 1984
Seghers, Pierre. *Le Livre d'or de la poésie française: des origines à 1940*. Marabout Université, 1976

Anthologie de la poésie chinoise classique. Poésie Gallimard, 1982
Anthologie de la poésie japonaise classique. Poésie Gallimard, 1978
Anthologie des poètes délaissés. Table Ronde, 1994
Chagrins d'amour. Le Cherche-Midi Editeur, 1992
A Cottage flora. Webb and Bower, Exeter, 1982
Les Fleurs dans la poésie française. Plon, 1954
Le Langage des fleurs. Éditions du Chêne, 1983
Le Langage des fleurs. Delarue éditeur
Green magic. The Viking Prell. New-York, 1977
Language of flowers. Hugh Evelyn, London, 1963
Les Plus beaux manuscrits des poètes français. Robert-Laffont, 1994
La Provence des peintres et des écrivains. Ed. Mermod, Lucerne, 1956
Le Temps qu'il fait. Albin-Michel, 1960